Space Exploration

Space Exploration

Edited by Nita Mallick

Britannica®
Educational Publishing

IN ASSOCIATION WITH

ROSEN
EDUCATIONAL SERVICES

Published in 2017 by Britannica Educational Publishing (a trademark of Encyclopædia Britannica, Inc.) in association with The Rosen Publishing Group, Inc.
29 East 21st Street, New York, NY 10010

Distributed exclusively by Rosen Publishing.
To see additional Britannica Educational Publishing titles, go to rosenpublishing.com

First Edition

Britannica Educational Publishing
J.E. Luebering: Executive Director, Core Editorial
Anthony L. Green: Editor, Compton's by Britannica

Rosen Publishing
Nita Mallick: Editor
Nelson Sá: Art Director
Brian Garvey: Designer
Cindy Reiman: Photography Manager
Karen Huang: Photo Researcher

Library of Congress Cataloging-in-Publication Data

Names: Mallick, Nita, editor.
Title: Space exploration / edited by Nita Mallick.
Description: New York : Britannica Educational Publishing in association with Rosen Educational Services, 2017. | Series: The study of science | Includes bibliographical references and index.
Identifiers: LCCN 2016020470 | ISBN 9781508104278 (library bound)
Subjects: LCSH: Outer space—Exploration—Juvenile literature. | Manned space flight—Juvenile literature.
Classification: LCC QB500.262 .S6232 2017 | DDC 629.45—dc23
LC record available at https://lccn.loc.gov/2016020470

Photo credits: Cover, p. 3 © iStockphoto.com/3DSculptor; pp. 8-9, 30-31, 53, 72, 75, 76, 79, 83, 97, 105 NASA; p. 13 The Hubble Heritage Team (AURA/STScl/NASA); p. 19 ullstein bild/Getty Images; p. 22 © Everett Collection Inc./Alamy Stock Photo; p. 24 Marshall Space Flight Center/NASA; pp. 27, 32, 35, 43, 50, 87, 92, 95 Encyclopædia Britannica, Inc.; p. 36 Gianni Woods/NASA; p. 40 Larry Mulvehill/ Science Source/Getty Images; p. 46 illustration adapted courtesy Encyclopædia Britannica, Inc.; p. 54 AdStock/Universal Images Group/Getty Images; p. 57 NASA/Goddard Space Flight Center; p. 63 Bill Ingalls/NASA/Getty Images; p. 66 Sovfoto/Universal Images Group/Getty Images; p. 84 © Sputnik/ Alamy Stock Photo; p. 100 NASA/Bill Ingalls; cover and interior pages backgrounds and borders © iStockphoto.com/LuMaxArt

Manufactured in China

CONTENTS

During the Apollo 11 mission in 1969, U.S. astronauts Neil Armstrong (*pictured above*) and Edwin ("Buzz") Aldrin became the first people to walk on the Moon.

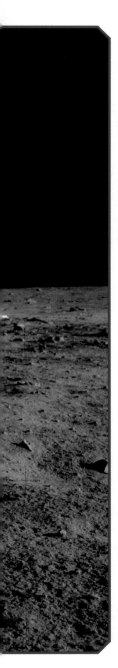

Humans have always looked at the heavens and wondered about the nature of the objects seen in the night sky. It was not until the 20th century, however, that the development of rockets and advances in other technologies made the exploration of outer space possible. Space exploration is among the most fascinating ventures of modern times. It has carried first instruments, then people themselves, beyond Earth's atmosphere, into a remoteness that until relatively recently was hardly known or understood. Although its borders already have been crossed, space still holds mysteries and, undoubtedly, surprises beyond number.

Space exploration has captured the minds of many people, not only aircraft pilots and scientists but also writers and artists. The strong hold that space travel has always had on the imagination may well explain why professional astronauts and laypeople alike consent at their great peril, in the words of Tom Wolfe in *The Right Stuff* (1979), to sit "on top of an enormous Roman candle, such as a Redstone, Atlas, Titan or Saturn rocket, and wait for someone to light the fuse." It perhaps also explains why space exploration has been a common and enduring theme in literature and art. As centuries of science fiction in books and more recently in films make clear, "one small step for [a] man, one giant leap for mankind" was taken by the human spirit many times and in many ways before Neil Armstrong stamped humankind's first footprint on the Moon.

The space age began on October 4, 1957, when the Soviet Union successfully launched the first artificial satellite, Sputnik 1, into orbit around Earth. Less than four years later, on April 12, 1961, Soviet cosmonaut Yury Gagarin became the first human being to travel in space, as he orbited Earth aboard the Vostok 1 spacecraft. Within less than 10 years of Gagarin's voyage, U.S. astronaut Neil Armstrong became the first person to set foot on the Moon, on July 20, 1969. These journeys were a climax to centuries of speculation and study and to decades of work on the practical problems of space exploration. They were also a prelude to several thousands of missions, both manned and unmanned, to investigate the reaches of space beyond Earth's atmosphere.

In addition to landing on the Moon, human crews have performed a variety of missions in near-Earth orbit, including living and working for periods on orbiting space stations. Unmanned space probes have landed on Earth's Moon and Saturn's moon Titan, on the planets Venus and Mars, and on asteroids. Space probes have also flown past all the planets. Moreover, unmanned spacecraft include sounding rockets and artificial satellites that have been used for scientific research, telecommunications, meteorology, photographic reconnaissance, navigation, and many other applications.

Achieving spaceflight enabled humans to begin to explore the solar system and the rest of the universe, to understand the many objects and phenomena that are better observed from a space perspective, and to use for human benefit the resources and attributes of the space environment. All of these activities—discovery, scientific understanding, and the application of that understanding to serve human purposes—are elements of space exploration, the story of which will be examined in the following pages.

CHAPTER 1

THE REALM BEYOND EARTH

S pace is the region beyond Earth's atmosphere. Its beginning is hard to define, because the atmosphere does not end abruptly but simply grows thinner and thinner with increasing height.

For humans, the conditions of space begin at about 45,000 feet (13,700 meters). Above this level, they require sealed, pressurized suits or a cabin for breathing. Winged, "air-breathing" jet aircraft can operate at sustained altitudes of a little more than 80,000 feet (24,000 meters). Balloons have risen to about 150,000 feet (45,700 meters). Rocket-powered aircraft, not requiring oxygen from the air, ascend to more than 354,000 feet (107,900 meters), or some 67 miles (108 kilometers), a level above 99 percent of the atmosphere.

At an altitude of about 100 miles (160 kilometers), satellites can orbit Earth. There, true space may be said to begin. The farther regions of space are described by the bodies that limit them. Cislunar

An image captured by the Hubble Space Telescope shows several galaxies.

space is the area between Earth and the Moon. Interplanetary space lies between the Sun and the planets of the solar system. Interstellar space lies between the stars of a galaxy. Intergalactic space—unimaginably huge—lies between the myriad galaxies of the universe.

Although it contains less matter per unit of volume than do the highest vacuums that can be produced in laboratories, space is far from empty. The vast reaches between major celestial bodies are permeated by radiation and swept by charged particles and matter ranging from large meteoroids to the tiny grains known as cosmic dust.

WHY EXPLORE SPACE?

Clearly, for humans and their machines space is a hostile environment. Great ingenuity and lavish expenditure of time, talent, and money are required to permit them to survive there. Yet, exploring space remains an important scientific endeavor.

A principal reason for the exploration of space is to extend knowledge about Earth, the solar system, and the universe beyond. Artificial satellites have yielded much new information about Earth. Observation posts above Earth's atmosphere permit astronomers

BY-PRODUCTS OF SPACE RESEARCH

As space technology progressed after World War II, a curious development occurred. From the research that produced the rocket motors, liquid propellants, space suits, and other necessities of spaceflight emerged by-products that no one had anticipated. These were unexpected applications—in medicine, industry, and the home—for materials, equipment, and services that had been created for use in space. Such by-products are called spin-offs or fallout. Only a few of the great many by-products can be named here.

Perhaps the best-known examples of spin-offs are found in hospitals and doctors' offices. Some of these stem from space medical research. Many are adaptations from other areas of space technology. Typical of spun-off implements is a sight switch that permits some disabled people to operate devices they could not otherwise use. They do this by using their eye movements to interrupt a light beam. The switch was developed to give astronauts a means of controlling their spacecraft while their arms and legs were rendered useless by high acceleration.

Many items developed in space research are now being used in factories, offices, and homes. Some may seem trivial; others have been of great benefit. A very valuable industrial application was found for an infrared Earth-horizon sensor developed to orient spacecraft. It continuously monitors ribbons of steel moving at up to 50 miles (80 kilometers) an hour and maintains the desired product thickness.

Fiberglass materials for rocket-fuel tanks are now employed to make lightweight, high-strength storage tanks, railway tank cars, and highway tankers. A magnetic hammer that originally served to eliminate small imperfections

(continued on the next page)

(continued from the previous page)

from metal surfaces of the Saturn V rocket is being adapted for use in the automotive and shipbuilding industries.

These represent only a very few of the valuable by-products that could be mentioned. There are, for example, an aluminized plastic blanket that can be folded small enough to be carried in a pocket; a cooler-smoking tobacco pipe, lined with a material developed for nuclear rocket engines; an ultrasonic testing device that can reveal hidden earthquake damage in masonry structures; and an improved caulking compound for tiles, derived from sealants used in spacecraft.

One of the most valuable contributions of aerospace technology to industry in general is a management technique called the systems approach, or systems engineering. With the aid of computers, this technique brings together all the elements of a complex project—people, money, materials—so that everything is ready at the optimum time. It has been applied to a variety of problems unrelated to space exploration. Among them are cancer research, hospital design and management, city planning, crime detection and prevention, pollution control, building construction, and transportation.

to observe radiation that does not penetrate Earth's atmosphere. Spacecraft voyaging far from Earth have gathered new data about the Moon and the planets.

The exploration of space also has immediate practical value. Meteorological satellites aid in weather forecasting. Communications satellites multiply international communications channels and make possible the intercontinental transmission of television. Navigation satellites guide ships. Military satellites perform vital reconnaissance. Geodetic satellites make possible maps of unprecedented accuracy. Finally, many products of space technology find employment on Earth.

Perhaps the greatest and most compelling reason for exploring space, however, is humanity's insatiable curiosity. Today's space explorers probe beyond their planet in response to the same irresistible lure of the unknown that impelled their predecessors to cross the oceans and the continents, to seek out Earth's poles, to ply the air, to climb the mountains, and to plunge to the depths of the sea.

THE PREHISTORY OF SPACE EXPLORATION

In a sense, the history of space exploration began when early humans first looked upward and wondered at what they saw in the sky. Wonder, as always, prompted a quest for knowledge. Beginning in ancient times, people studied the stars and their movements. As a realistic picture of the solar system and the

universe evolved, the urge to travel beyond Earth became stronger. That urge found its first expression in literature.

SCIENCE AND SCIENCE FICTION

Science fiction—usually thought of as a literary form of the 20th and 21st centuries—actually made its first appearance in the 2nd century CE. Most educated people of that period believed that the Moon was a solid body. The ancient Greek writer Plutarch, in his *On the Face That Appears in the Moon*, summed up the advanced views of his time. He held that the Moon was a smaller Earth. The idea of flight to the Moon was advanced in two stories written as early as 160 CE by Lucian of Samosata, a Greek. In Lucian's "True History" the hero is blown to the Moon during a storm. The hero of Lucian's "Icaro-Menippus" uses the wings of large birds.

During the Middle Ages no more stories of space travel were written. Late in the Renaissance, however, as scientific interests revived, interest in space also reawakened.

In the 17th century the invention of the telescope and the work of Johannes Kepler in Germany and Isaac Newton in England yielded knowledge of the solar system. Kepler

Johannes Kepler (1571–1630) is best known for discovering laws describing the motions of the planets in the solar system.

accurately described the orbits of the planets. Newton set forth mathematically the laws of gravitation and motion. He also broached the idea of an artificial satellite and calculated the escape velocity needed to leave Earth's gravitational field.

Kepler was an author of science fiction as well as an astronomer. His *Sleep*, a tale of a trip to the Moon, was published in 1634, after his death. The rocket as a device for space travel made its first appearance in a 1657 Moon-trip novel written by Savinien Cyrano de Bergerac of France.

Perhaps the most famous of space-travel novels, the French writer Jules Verne's *From the Earth to the Moon*, appeared in 1865. The idea of an artificial Earth satellite entered fiction in *The Brick Moon*, a magazine serial of 1869–70 by the American Edward Everett Hale. Hale's satellite was to be a navigational aid. The concept of manned artificial satellites remained a key theme in early 20th-century fictional works on space exploration.

PIONEERS OF SPACE EXPLORATION

Toward the close of the 19th century and in the first decades of the 20th century, science began to overtake fiction. In a number of countries serious attempts were made to solve the theoretical and technical problems of space exploration. During this period several individuals and groups made contributions that are still of value.

Konstantin E. Tsiolkovsky, a Russian schoolteacher, was among the foremost pioneer theoreticians. He was the first to derive the fundamental rocket equation, by means of which it is possible to calculate the ultimate velocity of a rocket if the mass of the rocket, the mass of its propellants, and the velocity of its exhaust are known. Tsiolkovsky also suggested the use of liquid fuels and of multistage, or step, rockets.

A second theoretician, Hermann Oberth, a German, had perhaps the greatest vision. Possibly because he sought publicity, Oberth's work had the greatest impact of all in exciting new interest in rocketry and space exploration. His first and most famous book, *The Rocket into Interplanetary Space*, was published in 1923. Like other pioneering works, it contained an exposition of the fundamentals of rocket propulsion. It also included proofs that a rocket can both operate in a vacuum and exceed the velocity of its own exhaust. Oberth also speculated upon the problems of manned spaceflight.

HERMANN OBERTH

The German scientist Hermann Oberth made many advances in rocketry. Along with Robert Goddard of the United States and Konstantin Tsiolkovsky of Russia, he is generally credited as one of the founders of modern astronautics. Unlike the others, Oberth lived to see space travel become a reality.

Hermann Julius Oberth was born on June 25, 1894, in Nagyszeben, Austria-Hungary (now Sibiu, Romania). After leaving military service in World War I, he studied at the University of Heidelberg, Germany. In 1923 he published a book, based on his university dissertation, that aroused public

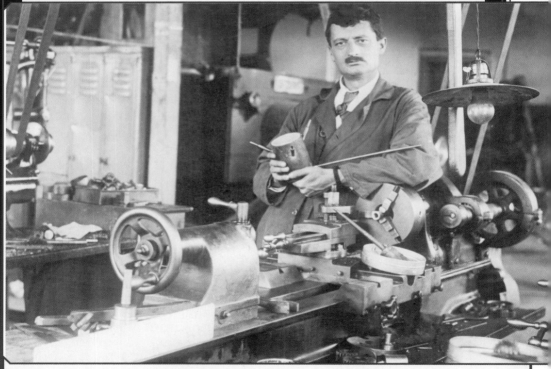

Hermann Oberth (1894–1989) was a pioneer of rocket science.

interest in space travel—even though the university had denied him a degree. The book explained how a liquid-fueled rocket could be made to go fast enough to enter space.

In 1930 Oberth patented a liquid-fueled rocket, which he later built and tested. One of his assistants was the young rocket scientist Wernher von Braun. In 1938 Oberth joined the faculty of the Technical University of Vienna, Austria. He became a German citizen in 1940 and went to work for Braun at the rocket center at Peenemünde, Germany, in 1941. In 1943 he began work on solid-fueled rockets.

After the end of World War II Oberth worked in West Germany, Switzerland, and Italy. In 1954 he published a book about space travel, which was later translated into English as *Man into Space*. In 1955 he rejoined Braun at the U.S. Army's Redstone Arsenal in Huntsville, Alabama. In 1958 he returned to Germany, and in 1962 he retired. He died on December 29, 1989, in Nürnberg, West Germany.

The work of U.S. physicist Robert Hutchings Goddard earned him the byname Father of Modern Rocketry. Early in life, through reading the works of Jules Verne and others, Goddard acquired an interest in space and its exploration that shaped his career. He devoted his life to rocket design.

Late in 1919 Goddard's most influential publication was issued by the Smithsonian Institution, which had in 1916 begun to subsidize his experimental work. Entitled *A Method*

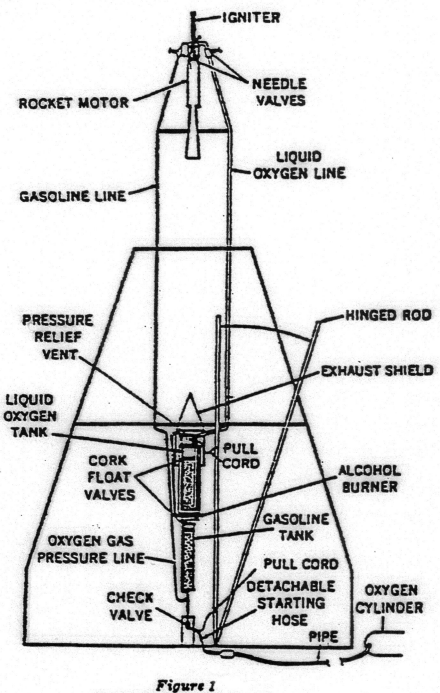

IGNITER

NEEDLE
VALVES

ROCKET MOTOR

LIQUID
OXYGEN LINE

GASOLINE LINE

HINGED ROD

PRESSURE
RELIEF
VENT

EXHAUST SHIELD

LIQUID
OXYGEN
TANK

PULL
CORD

CORK
FLOAT
VALVES

ALCOHOL
BURNER

GASOLINE
TANK

OXYGEN GAS
PRESSURE LINE

PULL CORD

DETACHABLE
STARTING
HOSE

OXYGEN
CYLINDER

CHECK
VALVE

PIPE

Figure 1
Dr. Goddard's 1926 Rocket

A diagram depicts Robert Goddard's liquid oxygen–gasoline rocket. The rocket—launched in 1926—flew for 2.5 seconds, reached an altitude of 41 feet (12.5 meters), and landed 184 feet (56 meters) away from the launch site.

of Reaching Extreme Altitudes, the booklet set forth the principles of rocketry in mathematical terms. It also furnished calculations of the rocket masses that would be required to lift loads to varying heights. One section—"Calculation of Minimum Mass Required to Raise One Pound to an 'Infinite' Altitude"—discussed the possibility of sending a rocket to the Moon.

Early in the 1920s Goddard began work on the development of liquid-propellant rockets. By 1926 he had developed a workable small motor. On the morning of March 16, in a field on his aunt's farm near Auburn, Massachusetts, Goddard launched the world's first successful liquid-propellant rocket—a spidery contrivance of tanks and tubes that rose to a height of 41 feet (12.5 meters) and traveled 184 feet (56 meters) horizontally.

Through the 1930s Goddard continued to develop liquid-propellant rockets, eventually producing models that reached heights of a mile and a half (2.5 kilometers). Goddard conceived and patented virtually all the fundamental components of modern rockets.

THE ROCKET SOCIETIES

In the 1920s and 1930s, inspired and guided by the work of the theoreticians and their

popularizers, rocket enthusiasts throughout the world formed societies to study the possibilities of space exploration. Many of the 20th century's most noted space scientists began their work in those groups.

The Soviet Union's Society for the Study of Interplanetary Travel was founded in 1924. After it was suppressed by the communist government, a second organization—the Group for the Study of Reactive Propulsion—was formed in 1931; ultimately it provided the nucleus of the Soviet government's rocket-research agency. By the mid-1930s the Soviet society had produced liquid-propellant sounding rockets that reached heights of about 6 miles (9.6 kilometers).

In the United States the American Interplanetary Society was formed in 1930. Later renamed the American Rocket Society, it joined the Institute of Aerospace Sciences in 1962 to form the American Institute of Aeronautics and Astronautics. During the 1930s members of the society built and tested a number of small liquid-propellant rockets. In England the British Interplanetary Society was formed in 1933. Space science also became an important study of the Astronomical Society of France.

The German V-2 missile, used as a weapon during World War II, was the forerunner of modern space rockets. It was developed through the efforts of scientists led by Wernher von Braun.

In Germany the Society for Space Travel was organized in 1927. Experiments conducted by the group in the 1930s paved the way for the development of the V-2. This ballistic missile, a weapon used against the Allies during World War II, contributed greatly to the production of today's space boosters. The principal developers of the V-2, led by Wernher von Braun, came to the United States after the war. Many of them played key roles in the engineering of U.S. military rockets and space vehicles.

In the years after World War II, spaceflight became an activity of governments. By that time it had become too expensive for private individuals, societies, or corporations to undertake.

CHAPTER 2

REACHING INTO SPACE

Despite the dream, it was many centuries before people could rise even a short distance above Earth's surface. The first steps toward exploring and traveling in space were taken with kites, balloons, and airplanes. With these devices, however, humans were still confined to Earth's atmosphere, because the devices all depend upon air for support—and the airplane requires oxygen from the air to burn its fuel. The advent of rockets and spacecraft finally extended the reach beyond the atmosphere. At last humans could live in orbiting space stations, visit the Moon, and send mechanical surrogates to the edge of the solar system and beyond.

NASA launched the New Horizons spacecraft aboard an Atlas V rocket in 2006.

THE ROCKET—
THE KEY TO SPACE

Flight above Earth's atmosphere requires a device that carries both its fuel and its oxidizer and that does not depend on the atmosphere for support. That device is the rocket, a reaction engine that operates in accordance with

Newton's third law of motion, which states that "for every action there is an equal and opposite reaction." A rocket is propelled by the forward push that results as a reaction to the ejection of exhaust gases from the back of the rocket at extremely high velocities.

Most of the rockets used in space exploration are multistage, or step, rockets, in which one rocket is placed atop another. Successive stages are discarded as they exhaust their propellants. This process increases the efficiency of the vehicle because, as each empty stage falls away, the mass that must be accelerated by the remaining stages is reduced.

The power of a rocket is called its thrust. In the United States thrust is usually expressed in pounds. The hot gases that provide the thrust and drive a rocket are produced by the combustion of the rocket's propellants—fuel and oxidizer. Propellants may be either solid or liquid. Solids are easier to handle and store

Liquid Propellant

Solid Propellant

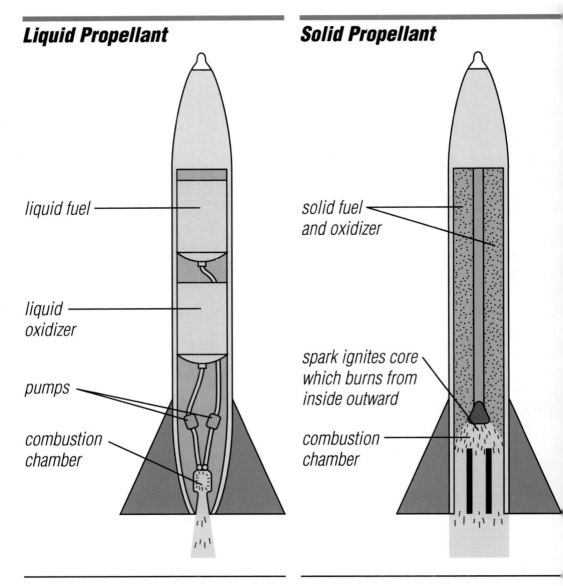

liquid fuel

liquid oxidizer

pumps

combustion chamber

solid fuel and oxidizer

spark ignites core which burns from inside outward

combustion chamber

rocket003a4

Most rockets use either solid or liquid chemical propellants. In most liquid-propellant systems, the fuel and oxidizer are pumped from separate tanks into the combustion chamber. Solid-propellant systems carry the fuel and oxidizer already mixed together in a solid state.

than are liquids, but liquids produce more thrust per pound of propellant and they can be throttled—that is, their thrust can be varied. Liquid propellants, therefore, are generally used for space vehicles. A common combination is liquid oxygen as the oxidizer and heavy hydrocarbons (such as kerosene) or liquid hydrogen as the fuel.

Although chemical rockets initially were considered too inefficient to propel large manned spacecraft on long flights, technological advances made them one of the most common types of rockets in the 20th and 21st centuries. With further development, nuclear-fission and nuclear-fusion engines may be used widely in the future.

SOUNDING ROCKETS AND LAUNCH VEHICLES

The rockets used in space exploration today may be divided into two groups: sounding rockets and launch vehicles. Sounding rockets are named for explosives that were once used to sound the atmosphere. These rockets carry instruments into the upper atmosphere and space to conduct experiments. Ordinarily the instrument package is detached at the desired altitude and returns to Earth by parachute.

Data may be stored on board for later playback or telemetered as the package descends.

Sounding rockets are useful for studying the atmosphere between about 20 and 100 miles (30 and 160 kilometers) above Earth. At these altitudes the air is too thin to support balloons or aircraft but too dense to allow satellites to orbit for more than a few days. Sounding rockets also provide a means of carrying out space-science research and observations for less than the cost of a satellite. They allow graduate students to have ready access to space in order to carry out basic experiments. In addition, less wealthy nations that cannot afford to orbit satellites or send spacecraft to the Moon and planets can have modest space-research programs using sounding rockets. A typical U.S. sounding rocket used in astronomy and astrophysics research is the Nike–Black Brant. This two-stage vehicle is about 46 feet (14 meters) long and can carry a payload of up to 1,200 pounds (545 kilograms).

Launch vehicles are rockets that are used to propel spacecraft into Earth orbit or to boost them beyond Earth's vicinity. The earliest launch vehicles were derived from the ballistic missiles developed by the United States and the Soviet Union after World War II. Modified Atlas intercontinental ballistic missiles launched the one-man Mercury spacecraft.

Modified Titan II missiles sent the two-man Gemini spacecraft into orbit. Vostoks—the Soviet Union's first manned spacecraft—were launched into orbit by derivatives of a Soviet intercontinental missile. Many later launch vehicles were developed specifically for space exploration and not as weapons. France was the third country to launch a satellite, in the mid-1960s, and Japan, China, and the United Kingdom each launched one in the early 1970s.

A great variety of launch vehicles have been developed. Some have lifted a cargo of

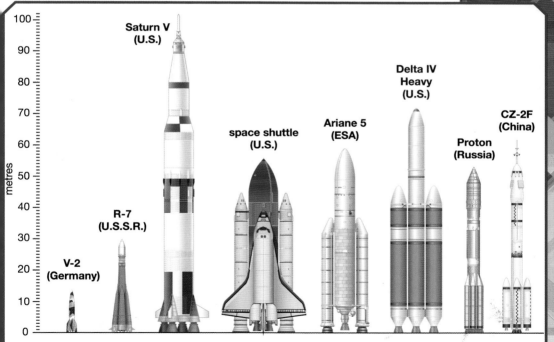

The diagram compares eight launch vehicles. The German V-2 and the Soviet R-7 were developed as weapons, though the R-7 was also used as a space launch vehicle. The other vehicles shown were developed for space exploration.

MAJOR ROCKET-LAUNCHING CENTERS

For reasons of safety, space-launch centers are usually located so that rockets may be fired over large open spaces— either oceans or sparsely populated land. Among the world's largest launch centers in regular use are those in the United States and Russia's complex in Kazakhstan. Other major launch facilities include the French Space Agency's ESA-sponsored site at Kourou, French Guiana, and Japan's site at Kagoshima.

The principal U.S. center, commonly called Cape Canaveral, is on the Atlantic coast of Florida, some 60

A space shuttle is launched at Cape Canaveral in Florida.

miles (95 kilometers) east of Orlando. Personnel at the major installation, the John F. Kennedy Space Center of the National Aeronautics and Space Administration (NASA), and the U.S. Air Force's 45th Space Wing at Patrick Air Force Base work closely together. Cape Canaveral's principal facilities include a headquarters, a flight crew training building, a manned-spacecraft operations building, and a central instrumentation facility. In the center's huge Vehicle Assembly Building the 363-foot-tall Saturn V rockets, used in Project Apollo, were assembled on a mobile launcher. The Kennedy Space Center is on Merritt Island. NASA's Lyndon B. Johnson Space Center, near Houston, Texas, controls manned space missions after liftoff.

Cape Canaveral proper—formerly Cape Kennedy—is separated from Merritt Island by the Banana River. Both NASA and the Air Force maintain launch complexes on the cape. These are employed in the launching of various scientific and military satellites and deep-space probes. The cape also has facilities for the testing of military missiles.

Baikonur, the principal Russian (and formerly Soviet) space-launch complex, is also a center for the launching of intercontinental ballistic missiles and other military missiles. The complex is located near the town of Tyuratam, east of the Aral Sea on the steppes of Kazakhstan. The missile-launching facilities, largely underground, are widely dispersed throughout the desert. Space-launching pads, however, are above ground. The supporting facilities are similar to those at Cape Canaveral and at Houston.

Both the United States and Russia have large military launching sites in addition to Cape Canaveral and Baikonur. In the United States these sites include the 30th Space Wing

(continued on the next page)

(continued from the previous page)

at Vandenberg Air Force Base, near Lompoc, California, and the U.S. Army's White Sands Missile Range in southern New Mexico. The civilian NASA maintains an installation on Wallops Island, Virginia, from which small satellites are orbited.

In Russia there is a major military facility at Kapustin Yar, near Volgograd north of the Caspian Sea. Another chief launch facility within Russia is located near Plesetsk, some 125 miles (200 kilometers) south of the White Sea port of Archangel.

only a few pounds while others have launched satellites, probes, shuttles, and enormous payloads such as the Skylab and Soyuz space stations. While most launch vehicles use liquid propellants, some are driven by solid propellants and others have both liquid- and solid-propellant stages. The Ariane launch vehicles of the European Space Agency (ESA) can place two satellites in orbit at a time. Vehicles of the two-stage Ariane 5 series use solid or liquid propellants for the first stage and liquid hydrogen and liquid oxygen for the second. Solid-propellant booster rockets help the vehicle achieve greater thrust at liftoff and then detach and fall to Earth after use. The manned, partially reusable

U.S. space shuttles carried the propellants for the main engines—liquid hydrogen and liquid oxygen—in an external tank that was discarded after the engines cut off. This allowed the shuttle's orbiter to be smaller than if the propellants were carried inside. Two strap-on, solid-propellant booster rockets also fired at launch; they parachuted back to Earth afterward for reuse.

SPACECRAFT LAUNCHING OPERATIONS

The process of launching a spacecraft starts weeks or months ahead of time with the assembly of the instruments that will perform the experiments or operations of the mission. This integration normally takes place in several phases, in which technicians connect the components and make sure that they work together. The components are also tested under conditions that simulate actual flight conditions. While the spacecraft's instrumentation is being assembled, the components of the launch vehicle are also assembled and tested in a similar process. The final phase of integration is to mate the spacecraft and

In 2014 the classic Kennedy Space Center countdown clock was retired and replaced with a flat screen device. The retired clock was placed outside the Space Center's visitor complex and restarted in March 2016.

launcher and exercise them in a countdown demonstration.

The spacecraft and launch vehicle are usually mated at or near the launching pad, the sturdy base that supports the rocket before it is launched. Beside the pad is a scaffold, called the gantry, from which the rocket and its payload are serviced.

Prelaunch operations are carried out according to a schedule known as the countdown. This is similar to the checklist followed by an airline pilot, but it is far more complex and involves many more participants. It is designed to ensure the safety of the ground crew and astronauts (if any), avoid unnecessary wear on equipment, permit the launch to take place at the planned time, and ensure that tracking and recovery systems are working properly and are coordinated.

Time preceding the launch is known as minus time, or T-minus. Varying with the complexity of the vehicle and its mission, the total length of minus time in a countdown ranges from a few hours to several days. T-time, or T-zero, is the time scheduled for liftoff. After that point the time is counted up in mission elapsed time (MET).

Ordinarily the launch director may hold a countdown at any point if there is a problem. Some countdowns may have built-in hold periods at specific points to allow time to correct the minor malfunctions that almost inevitably occur. The terminal count—the final period of the countdown—is normally controlled by computers because many of the scheduled events require responses that are faster than humanly possible. Nevertheless, the computer follows conservative rules set by humans.

CHAPTER 3

SPACECRAFT FUNDAMENTALS

S ince the orbiting of the first artificial Earth satellite—the Soviet Union's Sputnik 1—on October 4, 1957, thousands of spacecraft have been launched to perform a great variety of tasks. However varied they may be in purpose, all spacecraft move through space in accordance with fundamental physical laws, and all are made up of similar basic components.

FLIGHT TRAJECTORIES

The paths of spacecraft are governed by the laws of gravitation and planetary motion first set forth by Newton and Kepler. They are the same laws that govern the motion of all bodies in the universe— for instance, the Moon around Earth, and Earth around the Sun. The curved path that a spacecraft follows in space is called a trajectory. If the trajectory is closed and repetitive, it is considered an orbit and the spacecraft is called a satellite.

The body about which the satellite orbits, such as Earth or another planet, is called the satellite's primary. A satellite is held in orbit around its primary by the interaction of its own inertia and the gravitational attraction between it and the primary. Inertia tends to keep a satellite moving in a straight line. Gravitation tends to deflect it from that straight line and cause it to follow a curved path. If the curvature of the path parallels the curvature of the primary, the satellite will remain in orbit. In effect, the surface of the primary "falls away"

Why A Satellite Stays In Orbit

A small body (such as a satellite), if simply released, will fall directly toward a larger body, or primary (such as Earth) (A). If given a horizontal velocity as well, the small body will reach the primary at a point removed from the line of direct fall (B). The greater its horizontal velocity, the farther the small body will travel (C). If the small body has sufficient horizontal velocity, the curvature of its path will match the curvature of the surface of its primary, and it will stay in orbit about the primary (D).

from the satellite just as fast as the satellite falls toward the surface.

A satellite and its primary actually revolve around their common center of gravity. If, however, the mass of the satellite is very small in comparison with the mass of the primary, the center of gravity of the primary may be regarded as the point around which the satellite orbits, and approximate calculations of orbital characteristics are then greatly simplified.

The minimum velocity required to sustain a satellite in orbit around a primary would produce a circular orbit. It is called the circular velocity, and it may be expressed by the equation

$$V = \sqrt{\frac{GM}{R}}$$

in which V is the velocity, G the universal constant of gravitation, M the mass of the primary, and R the radius of the orbit, measured from the center of gravity of the primary. For the common U.S. units of miles and minutes, with mass in slugs, $G = 8.4 \times 10^{-16}$. Slugs are found by dividing the weight in pounds by the acceleration due to gravity—approximately 32.17 feet per second per second. For the metric units of kilometers and minutes, with mass in kilo-grams, $G = 2.4 \times 10^{-16}$. For Earth orbits, the circular-velocity equation may be simplified to

$$V = \frac{K}{\sqrt{R_e - h}},$$

in which K is the square root of GM (1.85×10^4 for the U.S. units, 3.78×10^4 for the metric), R_e is the radius of Earth (about 3,960 miles, or 6,370 kilometers), and h is the height of the orbit above the surface of Earth. (The mass of Earth is 4.08×10^{23} slugs, or 5.96×10^{24} kilograms.) It may be seen, for instance, that the velocity required to sustain a satellite in circular Earth orbit at the minimum practical height of about 100 miles (160 kilometers) is some 290 miles per minute, or 17,400 miles (28,000 kilome-ters) per hour.

For several reasons—including the diffi-culty of precise adjustment of velocity—exactly circular orbits are not achieved in practice. Noncircular orbits are elliptical, with the pri-mary at one focus of the ellipse. The closest point to Earth of a satellite in elliptical orbit is the perigee; the greatest distance, the apogee. Elliptical orbits result when the velocity of the

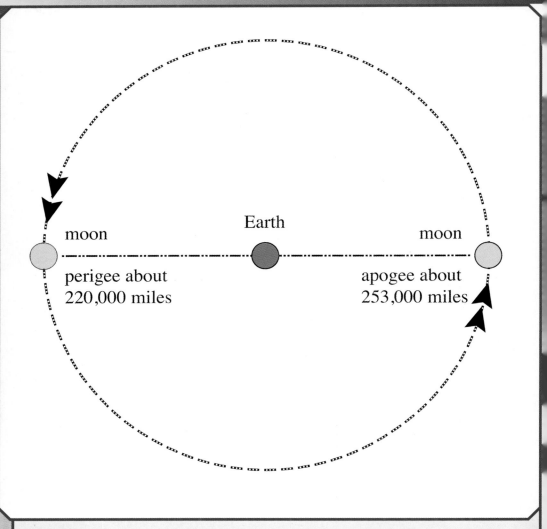

moon

Earth

moon

perigee about
220,000 miles

apogee about
253,000 miles

The Moon's orbit around Earth, like that of other Earth satellites, is an ellipse. The maximum distance between Earth and the Moon is called the apogee. The minimum distance is the perigee.

satellite at perigee is greater than the circular velocity for that height.

The velocity of a satellite at any point in an elliptical orbit may be determined by

$$V = \sqrt{GM\left(\frac{2}{R} - \frac{1}{a}\right)}$$

where R is the distance from the satellite to the center of gravity of the primary (R_e + h, for Earth orbits) and a is one half the major (long) axis of the ellipse (R_e plus half the sum of apogee and perigee, for Earth orbits). The velocity at perigee is

$$V_{per} = \sqrt{GM\left(\frac{2a - R}{aR}\right)}$$

and the velocity at apogee is

$$V_{apo} = \sqrt{GM\left(\frac{GMR}{a(2a - R)}\right)}$$

In both of these equations, R is the distance from the perigee to the center of the primary. Again, for Earth orbits, $\sqrt{GM} = K$.

The time required for a satellite to complete one sidereal, or Keplerian, orbit (defined in reference to the "fixed," or apparently motionless, stars in distant space) is called its period. For a circular orbit, the period is

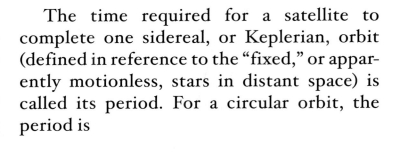

$$P = 2\pi\sqrt{\frac{R^3}{GM}}$$

For an elliptical orbit, the period is

$$P = 2\pi\sqrt{\frac{a^3}{GM}}$$

Thus, the time required to complete a circular Earth orbit 100 miles (160 kilometers) high would be about 1 hour 28 minutes. Interestingly, a satellite in a nearly circular orbit some 22,300 miles (35,900 kilometers) above Earth's equator will have a period of 24 hours—the time required for Earth to rotate once on its axis—and will appear to hover motionless above one point on Earth. Such an orbit is called a synchronous orbit.

During the flights of manned Gemini space-craft, the term "revolution" was introduced. The period of a revolution is the time elapsed between successive passes over a given meridian of Earth longitude. It is called the synodic period. The synodic period of a satellite will usually differ from its sidereal period because Earth rotates beneath the satellite. The time difference is influenced by the height of the orbit, its inclination (the angle between the plane of the orbit and that of the equator), and whether it is posigrade (in the direction of Earth's rotation) or retrograde (against that direction).

As the velocity of a satellite at a given perigee is increased, the ellipse of its orbit will become more and more eccentric. When the eccentricity reaches unity, the orbit is no longer a closed path, but an open-ended parabola. A spacecraft in a parabolic trajectory will not return to its primary; it has sufficient inertia to overcome the gravitational attraction of the primary and continue on, or escape, into space. Thus the velocity required to place a spacecraft into a parabolic trajectory is called the parabolic velocity, or escape velocity. At any given height above a primary, the parabolic velocity is $\sqrt{2}$ (approximately 1.414) times the circular velocity. Escape velocity from Earth's surface, then, is about 420

Velocity and Path

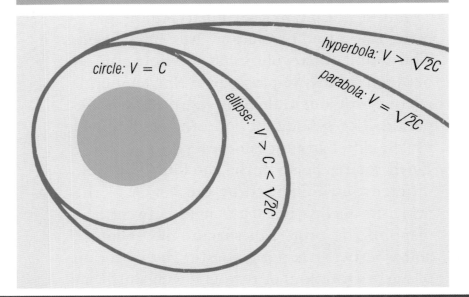

circle: V = C

hyperbola: V > √2C

parabola: V = √2C

ellipse: V > C < √2C

The minimum velocity (V) required to sustain a spacecraft in orbit is called the circular velocity (C). If V is greater than C but less than 2 multiplied by C (2C), the orbit will be elliptical. When V equals 2C, the eccentricity of the eclipse becomes unity, and the flight path of the spacecraft is no longer closed; the flight path is now a parabola. The spacecraft has reached escape velocity and will not return to its primary. Velocities greater than 2C produce hyperbolic paths.

miles per minute, or 25,000 miles (40,000 kilometers) per hour. For various reasons, however, actual escape trajectories are hyperbolic curves. A hyperbolic path is produced by any velocity greater than √2 times the circular velocity.

The fundamental relations given above consider only the gravitational attraction between a spacecraft and its primary. When applied, for example, to the data of an actual satellite in Earth orbit, they will yield results that are approximately correct, but not exact. Such a spacecraft would actually be influenced, for instance, by the gravity of the Sun and the Moon as well as by that of Earth. The equations that describe actual spacecraft motions are very complex. No general solutions are known, but they may be solved to any desired degree of accuracy by successive-approximation methods.

Types of Spacecraft

Spacecraft are designed to serve a variety of functions. The basic kinds of craft include sounding rockets, artificial satellites and space probes, space stations, and other vehicles for carrying humans through space. Sounding rockets carry scientific instruments into the upper atmosphere to collect data. An artificial satellite is a craft that orbits a larger astronomical body, such as Earth, its Moon, or other planets. Any spacecraft, manned or unmanned, that travels beyond Earth and escapes its gravitational field can be considered a space probe. If the probe travels beyond the reaches of Earth and its Moon, it is called a deep-space probe, and if it visits other planets, it is also considered a planetary probe. Lunar probes visit the Moon. Lunar and planetary

probes are variously designed to fly by, crash on, orbit, or land softly on their targets. Probes sent to explore the gaseous outer planets may be designed to collect data while parachuting through the outer atmosphere.

Manned spacecraft are among the most complex devices ever built, considering the diversity of tasks they must perform and the safety requirements that must be built in. Spacecraft that carry human crews have taken many forms, but all have had to provide both transportation and the means to sustain life.

Space stations are large orbiting spacecraft on which humans live and work for extended periods. The station's crew may conduct a variety of missions, such as military reconnaissance; gathering data on Earth, the Sun, or other astronomical objects; or conducting scientific experiments on how materials and biological systems behave in the virtual absence of gravity. Smaller stations, such as the Salyut and Skylab stations, have been launched fully assembled. Larger units, such as Mir and the International Space Station, have been sent up in several separate modules and assembled in orbit.

Space agencies often create a series of spacecraft that are similar in design or function or both. These craft may be grouped into

Crews from three countries have a meal in the Zvezda module of the International Space Station in 2001.

program families, such as Explorer, Apollo, Voyager, and Navstar in the United States; Soyuz, Venera, Salyut, and Gorizont in the Soviet Union (later Russia); SPOT in France; and Meteosat designed by the European Space Agency. The U.S. Apollo spacecraft of the 1960s and '70s, for example, were all part of the U.S. program to land on the Moon. The individual Apollo missions and their craft were designated by numbers, such as Apollo 7, Apollo 11, and Apollo 13. The Apollo spacecraft included command and service modules as well as a detachable lunar module. The command module was the crew's basic working and living area, while the service module provided propulsion, power, and storage for consumables. The detachable lunar module had its

In this 3D rendering, a weather satellite flies over a hurricane. Weather satellites are an example of applied spacecraft.

own rocket power to carry the crew to land on the Moon.

Satellites and probes may also be differentiated by their basic function. Working, or applied, spacecraft have utilitarian tasks, such as in communications, meteorological, geodetic, navigation, and military applications. Communications satellites relay radio and television signals. Meteorological, or weather, satellites send cloud-cover pictures and other data. Geodetic satellites make possible maps of greater accuracy. Navigation satellites help ships find their way. Military satellites perform photographic and electronic reconnaissance.

Scientific spacecraft are designed to gather information on physical phenomena in space. They may carry a human crew that conducts experiments on board the craft or outside it. Unmanned scientific spacecraft carry instruments to obtain data on a variety of phenomena, including radiation, magnetic and gravitational fields, and astronomical bodies such as stars, planets, moons, asteroids, and comets. Smaller, mobile robotic probes can be deployed when the spacecraft reaches its target. For example, NASA's Pathfinder spacecraft, which landed on Mars on July 4, 1997, released a six-wheeled robotic rover called Sojourner onto the planet's surface, where it collected

MARS EXPLORATION ROVER

A pair of U.S. robotic vehicles both known individually as the Mars Exploration Rover explored the surface of Mars beginning in January 2004. The mission of each rover was to study the chemical and physical composition of the surface at various locations in order to help determine whether water had ever existed on the planet and to search for other signs that the planet might have supported some form of life.

The twin rovers, Spirit and Opportunity, were launched on June 10 and July 7, 2003, respectively. Spirit touched down in Gusev crater on January 3, 2004. Three weeks later, on January 24, Opportunity landed in a crater on the equatorial plain called Meridiani Planum on the opposite side of the planet. Both six-wheeled 40-pound (18-kilogram) rovers were equipped with cameras and a suite of instruments that included a microscopic imager, a rock-grinding tool, and infrared, gamma-ray, and alpha-particle spectrometers that analyzed the rocks, soil, and dust around their landing sites.

The landing sites had been chosen because they appeared to have been affected by water in Mars's past. Both rovers found evidence of past water; perhaps the most dramatic was the discovery by Opportunity of rocks that appeared to have been laid down at the shoreline of an ancient body of salty water.

Each rover was designed for a nominal 90-day mission but functioned so well that operations were extended several times. NASA finally decided to continue operating the two landers until they failed to respond to commands from Earth. In August 2005 Spirit reached the summit of Husband Hill, 269 feet (82 meters) above the Gusev crater plain. Spirit and Opportunity continued to work even after a significant Martian dust storm in 2007 coated their solar cells. Opportunity entered Victoria crater, an impact crater roughly 2,600 feet (800 meters) in

An artist's rendering shows the Opportunity rover on Mars. Opportunity and its former twin rover, Spirit, have provided scientists with invaluable information about the planet's surface and environment.

diameter and 230 feet (70 meters) deep, on September 11, 2007, on the riskiest trek yet for either of the rovers. On August 28, 2008, Opportunity emerged from Victoria crater and set off on a 7-mile (12-kilometer) journey to the much larger (14 miles [22 kilometers] in diameter) Endeavour crater.

In May 2009 Spirit became stuck in soft, sandy soil; its wheels were unable to gain any traction. Scientists on Earth strove unsuccessfully for months to free the rover, and in January 2010 NASA decided that Spirit would work from then on as a stationary lander. The rover had traveled more than 4.8 miles (7.7 kilometers) in its mobile lifetime. Spirit ceased transmitting to Earth on March 22, 2010, and NASA ended its mission on May 25, 2011. Opportunity continued to operate, and by 2016 it had driven more than 26 miles (42 kilometers).

data on the rocks and soil near the landing site. Engineers back on Earth controlled the rover's movements through a remote-control device. NASA's rovers Spirit and Opportunity began exploring the red planet's surface in 2004.

BASIC SUBSYSTEMS

Any spacecraft may be considered as a single system composed of several subsystems—an assembly of components, which, together, can perform a desired task. A number of basic subsystems are common to most spacecraft, regardless of their missions. Among these are power supply; onboard propulsion; environmental control; attitude control; onboard computer; guidance and control; instrumentation; communications; and structure.

POWER, PROPULSION, AND ENVIRONMENTAL CONTROL

The power-supply subsystem provides the electricity for other subsystems. In satellites that will be in orbit for extended periods, the power often is generated by solar cells, which convert energy from the Sun into electricity. They are lightweight, reasonably inexpensive, reliable, and long-lived—all essential requirements for a spacecraft power subsystem. Batteries—recharged by the solar cells—may provide power when the solar cells are in the dark.

Thermoelectric power supplies, employing radioisotopes as heat sources, have been used in some satellites. They are long-lived but expensive. Fuel cells, in which oxygen and hydrogen are combined to yield electricity, water, and heat, are used in U.S. manned spacecraft.

The onboard propulsion subsystem is variously employed to change the orbit of a satellite or the trajectory of a probe, to "keep station" with other objects, to remove a spacecraft from orbit, or to brake a probe for landing. It consists of one or more liquid- or solid-propellant rockets.

The environmental-control subsystem protects spacecraft components and astronauts. The crew of a manned spacecraft must have oxygen to breathe, plus food, water, and some means of disposing of human waste. Cabin temperature and pressure must be kept within certain limits, and some shielding from radiation must be provided. The less complex subsystem of an unmanned spacecraft is usually designed to control temperature and radiation, to which some electronic components are as sensitive as are humans. Temperature control may be achieved by

reflective or absorptive external coatings or by such means as electric heaters.

ATTITUDE, COMPUTATION, AND GUIDANCE

The attitude-control subsystem keeps the spacecraft oriented with respect to an external reference. For example, solar cells must be kept pointed toward the Sun, communications antennas toward Earth, and cameras toward their subjects. Small rockets or compressed-gas jets are often used for attitude control. Magnets that interact with Earth's magnetic field also may be used. The subsystem usually responds to onboard sensors, such as gyroscopes or Sun- or star-trackers.

The onboard computer subsystem provides computing service for other subsystems. It may variously store engineering data, commands for other subsystems, and scientific data from sensors. It can also serve as an event timer, or clock.

The guidance-and-control subsystem monitors the spacecraft's attitude and velocity. It may also receive information from ground stations in order to issue to other subsystems the appropriate commands to keep the spacecraft in a desired orbit or other trajectory. The guidance-and-control, computer, and attitude-control subsystems are closely related.

INSTRUMENTATION, COMMUNICATIONS, AND STRUCTURE

The instrumentation subsystem is the data-gathering equipment of the spacecraft. Among the instruments that gather information outside the spacecraft may be cameras, radiation counters, and spectrometers. Instruments to collect information inside the spacecraft may include biomedical sensors that measure such phenomena as the temperatures and heartbeats of astronauts. Other instruments monitor the operation of the spacecraft itself.

The communications subsystem transmits and receives information by radio. Information transmitted includes data from scientific, biological, and engineering instruments. Commands are received from control stations on Earth to start or stop various functions of the spacecraft.

The structure, or skeleton, of a spacecraft may also be regarded as a subsystem. It supports and holds together the other subsystems.

GROUND SUPPORT FACILITIES

Information is received from—and transmitted to—spacecraft through elaborate networks of tracking stations on Earth. NASA, for example, has employed a variety of networks, such as the Manned Space Flight Network and the Space Tracking and Data Network (STDN), for communications with both manned and unmanned spacecraft.

To contact deep-space probes, NASA developed the Deep Space Network (DSN), which has stations near Canberra, Australia; at Goldstone, California; and near Madrid, Spain. To replace the STDN, NASA employed the Tracking and Data Relay Satellite System (TDRSS), which utilizes an array of satellites in geosynchronous orbit in contact with ground terminals at White Sands, New Mexico. NASA has used this system to track satellites in low orbit around Earth, including the U.S. space shuttles, the Hubble Telescope, and the International Space Station. The original fleet of six TDRSS satellites was launched in the 1980s and '90s, and three enhanced satellites were launched in 2000 and 2002. Third-generation satellites were launched in 2013 and 2014.

The mission control room at NASA's Jet Propulsion Laboratory in Pasadena, California, manages the Deep Space Network, an international system of giant antennas that collect data from interplanetary space probes.

The U.S. Department of Defense also operates space-tracking facilities to communicate with military spacecraft. The Soviet Union had a similar network of facilities across its territory. Many other countries also have tracking networks.

Chapter 4

Human Spaceflight

Human beings evolved on the surface of Earth and are naturally fitted for life on it or only a few feet above it. Space is an alien environment. In the journey into space, humans have overcome obstacles perhaps more formidable than any faced before.

Experiments with Animals

Before human beings first risked venturing into the hostile environment of space, animals were used in a variety of experiments to help determine whether biological organisms, properly protected, could survive spaceflight. Many of these experiments were conducted on Earth, but several involved sending animals into space aboard unmanned craft. The information gained through these experiments helped engineers design spacecraft in which people could not only survive but also function efficiently. Scientists also conducted experiments on animals to help investigate the effects of prolonged exposure to the conditions of spaceflight and the long-term risks associated with space travel.

In the United States the first use of rockets in biological research came in 1947, during tests of captured German V-2 ballistic missiles at the White Sands proving ground in New Mexico. Flights involving monkeys demonstrated that the animals could withstand the acceleration and brief periods of weightlessness. In the Soviet Union known experiments began in 1951 with the launching of a small dog in the nose cone of a sounding rocket.

On November 3, 1957, the Soviet Union became the first country to place a living creature in Earth orbit in an artificial satellite. The female dog Laika, accustomed by special training to the acceleration and noise of rocket flight, was launched in the satellite Sputnik 2. Instruments transmitted data on Laika's breathing, heartbeat, and blood pressure until the telemetry system failed about five hours after liftoff. No provision had been made for recovering the craft, and Laika died on board. That Laika survived the acceleration and tolerated a period of weightlessness

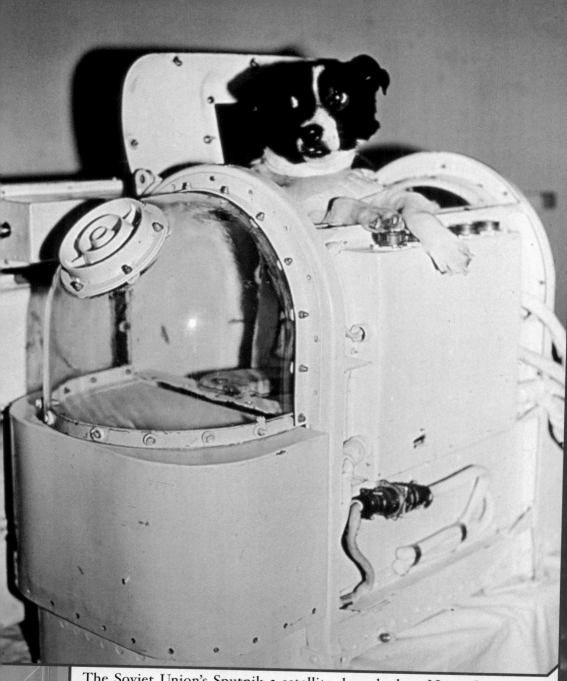

The Soviet Union's Sputnik 2 satellite, launched on November 3, 1957, carried the dog Laika, the first living creature to be shot into space and orbit Earth.

strongly suggested that humans too could function in space.

As the tempo of preparations for manned spaceflight increased in the Soviet Union and the United States, those countries sent a number of dogs and chimpanzees on spaceflights that orbited Earth. The journey of Enos, a chimpanzee, was typical of these flights. The 5½-year-old primate made two orbits in a U.S. Mercury spacecraft on November 29, 1961. While in flight, it ate, drank, and performed psychomotor tests for which it had been trained. Enos survived the mission and was safely recovered. Spaceflight had no apparent effect upon the animals' ability to bear normal offspring.

Of course, after human beings began traveling in space, important data were obtained by studying the human astronauts themselves. But, from the U.S. Biosatellite program of the late 1960s to experiments carried out aboard the U.S. space shuttles and the International Space Station in the late 20th and early 21st centuries, researchers continued to use the unique conditions of space to perform a wide variety of scientific experiments on living things of all kinds—including animals, plants, and microscopic organisms. In addition to conducting experiments relating specifically

Biosatellite Program

NASA's Biosatellite program launched a series of three U.S. Earth-orbiting scientific satellites designed to study the biological effects of weightlessness (zero gravity), cosmic radiation, and the absence of Earth's 24-hour day-night rhythm on plants and animals ranging from a variety of microorganisms to a primate. Such space laboratories were equipped with telemetering equipment with which to monitor the condition of the specimens. Biosatellite 1 (launched December 14, 1966) was not recovered because it failed to reenter Earth's atmosphere. Biosatellite 2 (launched September 7, 1967) was a complete success. It involved an assortment of biological experiments, including one concerned with mutations induced in the offspring of insects exposed to ionizing radiation in space. The flight of Biosatellite 3 (launched June 29, 1969), scheduled to last 31 days, had to be cut short when the trained pigtail monkey that was aboard became ill.

to space exploration, scientists have used the virtual absence of gravity to investigate an array of fundamental biological and physical processes.

Humans and Space

The barriers to manned spaceflight are both physical and psychological. They arise from both the nature of space and the means employed to reach space. These obstacles have been overcome by a combination of protective devices and rigorous training.

THE FUNCTIONAL BORDERS OF SPACE

The altitudes at which humans can no longer exist naturally are the functional borders of space. They are the heights at which various vital functions of the human organism fail to operate because of the nature of the ambient physical environment.

At an altitude of about 3 miles (5 kilometers) above Earth, humans suffer oxygen deficiency in the blood, or hypoxia, because of the low partial pressure of oxygen in the air. In order to thrive at this altitude, humans require an auxiliary supply of oxygen. Only 1.5 miles (2.4 kilometers) or so farther up, humans become subject to "the bends," or dysbarism. Nitrogen in the tissues is released because of the low atmospheric pressure. Bubbles collect in the blood and tissues, causing great pain and, in some cases, death.

Some 10 miles (16 kilometers) above Earth, humans experience anoxia, or an absence of oxygen in the body. At this altitude the atmospheric pressure is so low that the lungs can no longer exchange water vapor and carbon

dioxide for oxygen, even though there is oxygen in the air. A positive-pressure breathing apparatus is required. At an altitude of about 12 miles (19 kilometers), the atmospheric pressure is so low—about 47 millimeters of mercury—that it equals the vapor pressure of the fluids in the body. Bubbling of these fluids, or ebullism, from the eyes, mouth, nose, and other orifices occurs. A pressurized cabin or suit is necessary.

STRESSES AND HAZARDS OF SPACEFLIGHT

The people who travel into space successfully cross the functional borders because they are protected by the environmental-control subsystems of their spacecraft and space suits. They must, however, also overcome other stresses and hazards.

The first stress of spaceflight is acceleration, produced as the launch vehicle leaves the pad and rapidly builds up velocity. Within a few minutes after liftoff, for instance, the apparent weight of the astronauts of the U.S. Apollo missions increased from its usual value at Earth's surface (1g) to seven or eight times that value (7 or 8g). Acceleration affects voluntary muscular activity, blood circulation, and visual acuity.

Critical controls are therefore placed within easy reach of astronauts' couches. These are so placed that the astronauts lie on their backs, facing in the direction of flight. In this "eyeballs in" position, the heart can supply the brain with blood at accelerations of up to 10g, preventing dimming or loss of consciousness.

The same supine position is adopted during reentry, when high deceleration (negative acceleration) is experienced. Lighting of twice the normal intensity is provided during high acceleration to counteract dimming of vision.

Vibration and noise—primarily produced by rocket engines, propellant sloshing, engine movements, wind gusts, and air turbulence as the spacecraft passes transonic speed—can cause nausea, choking sensations, difficulty in breathing and seeing, headaches, and deafness. Although these stresses largely cease after the powered stage of flight, spacecraft and space suits are designed to attenuate noise and cushion vibration.

Temperature is also important. Humans can operate efficiently within only a narrow range of temperatures—about 50° to 80° F (10° to 27° C). Around 70° F (20° C) is ideal. Spacecraft must protect the astronauts and instruments from the extreme cold of space as well as the extreme heat generated upon reentry into the

A photo taken from the International Space Station in 2005 shows the thermal protection tiles under the nose of the space shuttle *Discovery*.

atmosphere. Temperature control is maintained both by powered heating-and-cooling systems and by such passive means as exterior coatings. Many spacecraft use ablative heat shields, which dissipate heat by charring and melting. They are not reusable, however, so they were not used on the space shuttles. Refractory coatings, which can withstand extreme temperatures directly without sustaining damage and which do not transmit heat to the craft's interior, have been used in the shuttles and some other spacecraft.

Radiation poses one of the greatest hazards to human beings in space. Exposure to high levels of radiation, including solar radiation, cosmic rays, X-rays, gamma rays, and many other types, can harm living cells. Excessive exposure may cause potentially fatal tumors and other serious health problems. Earth's magnetic field shields human beings from much harmful radiation. Nearly all manned space missions have taken place in near-Earth orbit, in which the spacecraft were still protected by Earth's magnetic field. The only exception has been the Apollo missions to the Moon, which were all of less than two weeks' duration. The Apollo flights also were carefully timed to avoid exposure to anticipated high levels of solar radiation. The spacecraft designs currently in use do not afford enough protection against radiation for humans to travel safely on long interplanetary missions. Spacecraft and space suits do screen out some forms of harmful electromagnetic radiation, such as nearly all the ultraviolet light, to which the eye is especially sensitive but to which the iris does not respond.

The possibility of sudden decompression, exposing the occupants of a spacecraft to the effects of extremely low pressures, is a further hazard. Small leaks may be detected by

sensors and, in some instances, repaired if necessary. Should repair be impossible, astronauts may have time to put on space suits. Sudden decompression—which could be caused, for example, by collision with a meteoroid—is probably not survivable by the occupants of present-day spacecraft. Fortunately, the chances that a spacecraft will strike an object large enough to cause explosive decompression are very small.

The effects of weightlessness, or the absence of virtually all sensation of acceleration, have not been fully evaluated. It is known, however, that weightlessness produces changes in human physiology. All space fliers have lost weight during their flights. Most space travelers regain the weight they lost within a day or two of their return to Earth.

Disorientation, greatly feared before the first manned spaceflights, occurred only once during the first eight years of manned flight. Soviet cosmonaut Gherman Titov, the second person to orbit Earth, became severely disoriented and mildly nauseated. Some later space fliers—particularly those who had little previous training or experience—had the sensation of being suspended upside down.

The loss of bone mass has proved a more widespread problem. During weightlessness,

Astronauts require customized equipment and a special workout regimen that accounts for the lack of gravity in order to maintain their strength while in space.

astronauts lose bone density at an accelerated rate, and it is difficult for them to regain the lost mass after returning from space. On long missions, the bones may become porous and brittle, as in a person with osteoporosis. Astronauts also lose mass in the calf and thigh muscles that on Earth are used to counter the effects of gravity. In addition, blood that normally pools in the legs and feet shifts to the upper regions of a person's body in the virtual absence of gravity. As a result, the face becomes puffy and the person experiences headaches and sinus congestion. As the body attempts to compensate, the total blood production decreases. For a few days after returning to Earth, many astronauts experience orthostatic hypotension, or low blood pressure when standing or sitting. This condition may cause light-headedness, dizziness, or fainting.

The limitations that weightlessness places upon physical activity are counteracted by various devices, including special handholds and footholds. Without such aids, a person attempting to turn a nut with a wrench would merely turn himself or herself, as he or she could offer no resistance to the force applied to the wrench. Compressed-gas jets have helped space travelers to maneuver outside their craft.

The unaccustomed environment of space may also produce psychological stresses. These are more difficult to define and evaluate—and probably more difficult to overcome—than are the

A space suit is a self-contained environment that must supply everything needed for an astronaut's life, as well as comfort.

physical stresses. Isolation could be an important psychological stress, but little is as yet known about the effects of long-term social, cultural, and perceptual isolation.

In the spaceflights conducted to date, isolation has produced no incapacitating mental stress—possibly because astronauts have been very busy and because they also have been in almost constant radio contact with Earth. Possible effects of isolation, however, include states of anxiety, indifference, exhilaration, and euphoria. Such reactions could be disastrous.

BECOMING AN ASTRONAUT

The men and women who have flown in space have been carefully selected and rigorously trained to withstand—and work efficiently in—the environment of space. The selection and training procedures for astronauts (called cosmonauts in Russia) are similar in most countries.

SELECTION

Candidates for space travel are selected from a wide field of applicants. Normally, a candidate must meet particular age and height

requirements, have at least a bachelor's degree or the equivalent in engineering, mathematics, or science, be in excellent physical and psychological health, and be a citizen of the selecting country. Astronauts or cosmonauts generally fall into one of two categories: pilots or scientists and engineers. A pilot candidate usually has extensive experience in flying high-performance aircraft and often has a military background. A scientist or engineer candidate, known as a mission specialist in the United States and a flight engineer in Russia, usually has a doctorate or its equivalent but does not need to be a pilot. The distinctions between these two types of space explorer have blurred somewhat with the development of long-duration space stations, because all members of their crews carry out station operations and experiments.

These two types of astronauts and cosmonauts generally undertake more than one space mission. At times, other scientists or engineers may join a particular mission to direct an experiment. Occasionally, civilians such as politicians, teachers, or journalists may be invited on a mission, or space tourists who can afford to pay huge sums of money may be allowed on board. These one-time space travelers are called payload specialists in the United States and guest cosmonauts in Russia.

TRAINING

Before being chosen for a mission, candidates undergo extensive training. The training programs generally combine academic studies, physical training, and aircraft piloting. Scientist and engineer candidates are trained to fly jet aircraft. Pilot candidates take basic courses in such areas as astronomy, geology, physiology, rocket propulsion, computer principles,

NASA astronauts work underwater at the Neutral Buoyancy Laboratory at Johnson Space Center in Houston, Texas. The huge water tank allows NASA to simulate weightlessness during astronaut training.

and celestial mechanics. Each astronaut also normally becomes a specialist in some area of space engineering associated with the spacecraft, launch vehicle, or tracking system.

Astronauts make use of a number of training devices. These include the human centrifuge, upon which they are accustomed to acceleration. Audiovisual devices assist in teaching astronauts to operate spacecraft subsystems. Weightlessness is introduced in aircraft flying ballistic paths and is simulated in neutral-buoyancy exercises underwater.

Once selected for a specific mission, each member of the crew for that mission begins an intensive training period. Much of the period is spent in very elaborate and realistic training devices. Mission simulators, for example, contain a cabin that looks exactly like the one in which the astronauts will fly. Instructors at consoles monitor the actions of the astronauts as they rehearse their mission. The computer relays problems to the astronauts through their instruments, notes their responses, and adjusts the instruments appropriately. The instructors and the computer also introduce emergencies to train the astronauts to respond correctly. In effect, people who fly in space have already been there many times.

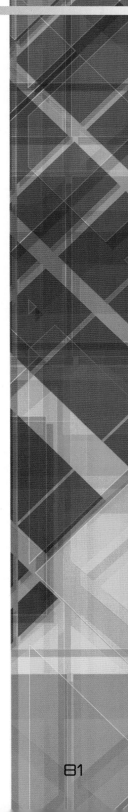

The training facilities are highly specialized, and there are only a few main astronaut training centers in the world. Within the United States, the principal training center is NASA's Johnson Space Center, in Houston, Texas. In Russia candidates are trained at the Yury Gagarin Cosmonaut Training Center (commonly called Star City), outside Moscow. The ESA trains its astronaut candidates at the European Astronaut Centre, in Cologne, Germany, while the training center for Japan's National Space Development Agency (NASDA) is Tsukuba Space Center, near Tokyo.

CHAPTER 5

MILESTONES IN HUMAN SPACEFLIGHT

The venture into space is perhaps the most complex and costly of all human undertakings. It is also surely among the most successful—less than two decades after the first brush of the edges of space, a human walked upon the Moon.

THE X-15 "SPACE PLANE"

The first crossing of the border of space was in a curious vehicle that was neither wholly spacecraft nor wholly airplane. It functioned as a manned rocket, capable of arcing briefly into the very lowest fringes of space, and as an airplane, landing with wings, rudder, stabilizer, and wheels. It was the X-15.

Conceived in the early 1950s and designed to reach altitudes of more than 50 miles (80 kilometers) and speeds of more than 4,000 miles (6,400 kilometers) per

An X-15 rocket-powered plane (*bottom*) is air-launched from a Boeing B-52 bomber. Flights of the experimental X-15 in the 1960s set unofficial altitude and speed records for piloted aircraft and contributed to the development of the U.S. manned spaceflight program.

hour, the X-15 first flew in September 1959. Three were built.

In nearly 200 flights between 1959 and the end of the program in 1968, the X-15 returned information that was of great value in the design of both spacecraft and supersonic aircraft. It reached an altitude of 67 miles (108 kilometers) and a speed of more than 4,500 miles (7,200 kilometers) per hour. Military pilots who flew the X-15 to heights of more than 62.5 miles (100.6 kilometers) were regarded as astronauts.

SOVIET MANNED SPACEFLIGHTS

The single-Earth-orbit flight of the Soviet Union's Yury Gagarin aboard the Vostok 1 spacecraft, on April 12, 1961, is regarded as the first true spaceflight. Five more flights of Vostok spacecraft followed. The last four were conducted in pairs. The first woman to fly in space, Cosmonaut Valentina V. Tereshkova, piloted Vostok 6.

Two flights of multiperson spacecraft—modified Vostoks dubbed Voskhod 1 and

In 1961 Soviet cosmonaut Yury Gagarin, aboard the Vostok 1, orbited Earth once in 1 hour and 29 minutes at a maximum speed of 17,000 miles (27,000 kilometers) per hour.

2—were made in 1964 and 1965. Voskhod 1 carried three men. Voskhod 2 carried two, one of whom—Cosmonaut Aleksey A. Leonov—became the first person to walk in space.

The more sophisticated Soyuz spacecraft was introduced in 1967. It was capable of docking. The flight of Soyuz 1 ended in tragedy when the craft's parachute lines tangled after reentry and the capsule plummeted to Earth, killing the sole occupant, Cosmonaut Vladimir M. Komarov—the first person killed in spaceflight.

The soundness of the Soyuz spacecraft was proved in October 1968 when the manned Soyuz 3 completed two rendezvous maneuvers with the unmanned Soyuz 2. Rendezvous, docking, and crew exchange were accomplished on Soyuz 4 and 5 in January 1969. In October 1969 Soyuz 6, 7, and 8 were launched; the mission was the largest group flight ever. In June 1970 Soyuz 9 set an endurance record of nearly 18 days.

In early 1971 the Soviets launched the world's first space station, Salyut 1. In June 1971 the Soyuz 11 crew boarded the station and stayed aboard for almost 24 days. The three men died during reentry, however; a leaky valve let the cabin air escape and asphyxiated the crew. As a

result of the tragedy, Soyuz missions were suspended until 1973.

In 1973 a Salyut 2 space station was launched but went unmanned; the Salyut 3 station in 1974 had two human crews. Further Soyuz missions continued and included dockings with additional Salyuts.

Salyuts 6 and 7 followed the same basic design as the earlier Salyuts but had improved systems and layouts. Salyut 6, launched in September 1977, was visited by 11 crews. With it the Soviets set and broke several endurance records. In addition, two upgraded Soyuz spacecraft were introduced—the unmanned Progress supply craft and the advanced two-person Soyuz T series. Salyut 7 was launched in April 1982. The crew of the Soyuz T-10 boarded the station and set a 237-day endurance record that ended in October 1984. They also went outside the spacecraft several times, in what is known as extravehicular activity (EVA), to improve and repair the station. One of the Salyut 7 guest crews included the second woman in space, Svetlana Y. Savitskaya, who became the first woman to walk in space.

The operations of Salyut 7 were largely ended in 1985. Soviet space activities focused on the new Mir space station, launched in February 1986 and equipped with a six-port

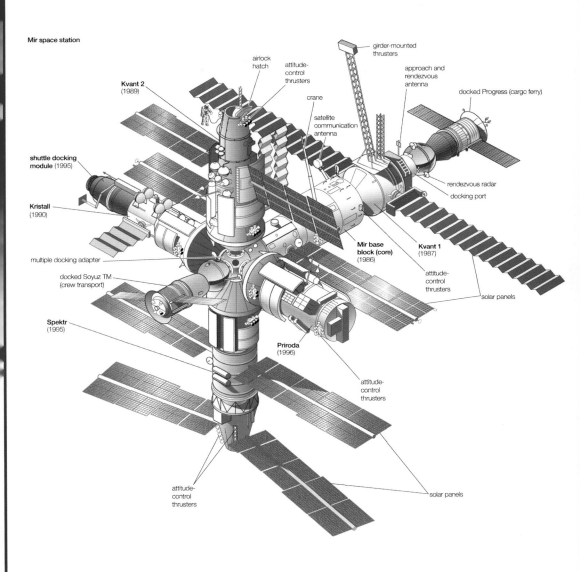

Mir space station

girder-mounted thrusters

airlock hatch

attitude-control thrusters

approach and rendezvous antenna

Kvant 2 (1989)

crane

satellite communication antenna

docked Progress (cargo ferry)

shuttle docking module (1995)

Kristall (1990)

rendezvous radar

docking port

multiple docking adapter

Mir base block (core) (1986)

Kvant 1 (1987)

attitude-control thrusters

solar panels

docked Soyuz TM (crew transport)

Spektr (1995)

Priroda (1996)

attitude-control thrusters

attitude-control thrusters

solar panels

A diagram depicts the Soviet/Russian space station Mir. The date shown for each module is its year of launch. Docked to the station are a Soyuz TM manned spacecraft and an unmanned Progress resupply ferry.

docking section. The Mir was boarded in 1986, for 123 days, by the Soyuz T-15 crew, and was visited by an unmanned model of the new Soyuz TM spacecraft.

In February 1987 the Soyuz TM-2 crew boarded Mir for a new record duration in space. Although Cosmonaut Aleksandr Laveikin became ill and was replaced by Cosmonaut Aleksandr P. Aleksandrov, mission commander Yury V. Romanenko remained aboard the station for a record-breaking 326 days, returning to Earth in December 1987. Another record was set in 1994–95, when Cosmonaut Valery Polyakov spent 438 days aboard the station.

In 1997 the space station experienced a series of near-catastrophes, including a fire within the space station's main module, a breakdown of the onboard oxygen-filtering system, and a collision with the Progress supply craft. The cargo ship tore a hole in one of the modules of the Mir station and damaged a solar panel. The damage to the spacecraft was extensive, forcing the crew to forgo a series of scheduled scientific experiments in an effort to preserve energy aboard the aging station, which had been designed to last only five years.

The events of 1997 created further uncomplimentary press for the beleaguered Russian space program. During the early years of space-flight and the heyday of the Soviet Union, it was hailed as the most advanced space program in the world, but it fell on hard times after the collapse of the Soviet Union in 1991. The Mir station, given its high-profile standing for more than a decade of service, seemed to many observers a symbol of the collapse of the Soviet space program. Finally, in late 1999, Mir was abandoned because of both a lack of funds to keep it operational and ongoing safety concerns. Its orbit deteriorated and it fell to Earth in March 2001.

United States Mercury and Gemini Flights

The first U.S. astronaut to enter space was Alan B. Shepard, Jr. His suborbital flight, on May 5, 1961, in a one-person Mercury spacecraft carried him 115 miles (185 kilometers) above Earth. On February 20, 1962, John H. Glenn, Jr., became the first American to orbit Earth. He completed three orbits in 4 hours 55 minutes. Three more flights completed the Mercury program.

The two-person Gemini vehicles were the world's first maneuverable manned space-craft. In the first manned Gemini flight—that of Gemini 3, on March 23, 1965—Virgil I. Grissom and John W. Young completed three orbits. On June 3, 1965, during the flight of Gemini 4, Edward H. White II became the first American to walk in space.

The first rendezvous between two orbiting spacecraft was accomplished on December 15, 1965. Walter M. Schirra, Jr., and Thomas P. Stafford maneuvered Gemini 6 to within a foot (30 centimeters) of Gemini 7, in which Frank Borman and James A. Lovell, Jr., set a spaceflight endurance record of 330 hours 35 minutes. In the succeeding Gemini flights, rendezvous and docking were achieved with unmanned Agena target vehicles. The program ended in November 1966 with Gemini 12.

Project Apollo: To the Moon

Mercury and Gemini were a prelude to Project Apollo, the goal of which was manned exploration of the Moon. Development of the three-person, three-module Apollo spacecraft and its massive Saturn V launch vehicle began in the early 1960s.

The first manned test of the Apollo spacecraft was scheduled for 1967, but in January 1967, during a practice countdown, Grissom, White, and Roger B. Chaffee were killed when a flash fire swept the command module in which they sat. The first manned Apollo spacecraft—Apollo 7—was launched on October 11, 1968. Schirra, Donn F. Eisele, and Walter Cunningham were in Earth orbit for 11 days.

In Apollo 8, launched on December 21, 1968, Borman, Lovell, and William Anders became the first people to orbit the Moon, completing 10 lunar orbits. Apollo 11, launched on July 16, 1969, carried the first humans to land on the Moon. Command pilot Neil A. Armstrong and lunar module pilot Edwin E. Aldrin, Jr., landed in the Mare Tranquillitatis on July 20 at 3:17 PM CDT. At 9:56 PM Armstrong stepped out of the lunar-landing vehicle *Eagle* and onto the Moon, uttering the now-famous words, "That's one small step for [a] man, one giant leap for mankind." He was followed by Aldrin. Michael Collins remained in the Moon-orbiting command module.

Apollo 12 launched on November 14, 1969, with a crew of Charles Conrad, Jr., Alan L. Bean, and Richard F. Gordon, Jr. Conrad

(From left to right) Neil Armstrong, Michael Collins, and Edwin ("Buzz") Aldrin of the Apollo 11 mission pose for a photo.

and Bean made the second successful lunar landing on November 19. Apollo 13 launched on April 11, 1970, but an explosion in an oxygen tank severely disabled the craft as it approached the Moon. Astronauts Lovell, Fred Haise, Jr., and John L. Swigert, Jr., moved to the lunar module during their return to Earth. Shepard and Edgar D. Mitchell made the third manned lunar landing on February

5, 1971, with Stuart A. Roosa orbiting in the Apollo 14 command module.

The fourth lunar landing was made on July 30, 1971, by the astronauts of Apollo 15. Using an electrically powered Lunar Roving Vehicle, the astronauts collected some 170 pounds (77 kilograms) of rocks and soil. The next landing took place on April 20, 1972, when crew members of Apollo 16 touched down in the rugged Descartes Highlands. They collected the first samples of lunar mountain soil and rocks.

Apollo 17, the last of the Apollo series, was launched on December 7, 1972. Two astronauts spent four days on the surface of the Moon and set up experiments to study the Moon's environment and interior.

Skylab, a 100-ton space laboratory, was launched into Earth orbit on May 14, 1973. The first crew—Conrad, Joseph P. Kerwin, and Paul J. Weitz, in a modified Apollo—docked with the lab on May 25, during the Skylab 2 mission. Their experiments included studies of the Sun, Earth resources, and the human body's reaction to an extended stay in space. Their space endurance record of 28 days was topped by the Skylab 3 crew, whose mission lasted 59 days, and by the Skylab 4 mission, which lasted 84 days.

SPACE SHUTTLE PROGRAM

During the 1970s the United States developed the space shuttle, the first reusable manned space vehicle. It combined three systems: a winged orbiter carrying crew and payload; an external tank with propellant for the three main rocket engines; and twin solid rocket boosters to lift the craft above the thickest part of the atmosphere. About two minutes after liftoff, the boosters detached and parachuted back to Earth, usually into the ocean, for recycling. By the time the orbiter reached about 99 percent of its orbital velocity, the propellants in the external tank had been used up, and the tank was jettisoned. Unlike the other two major shuttle components, the external tank was not reused; it disintegrated upon reentering the atmosphere. The orbiter made an unpowered descent at the end of the mission, gliding to a landing on a runway.

The program was formally called the Space Transportation System (STS). The fleet began with a total of four space shuttles; they were named for famous oceangoing ships: *Columbia*, *Challenger*, *Discovery*, and *Atlantis*.

U.S. space shuttle

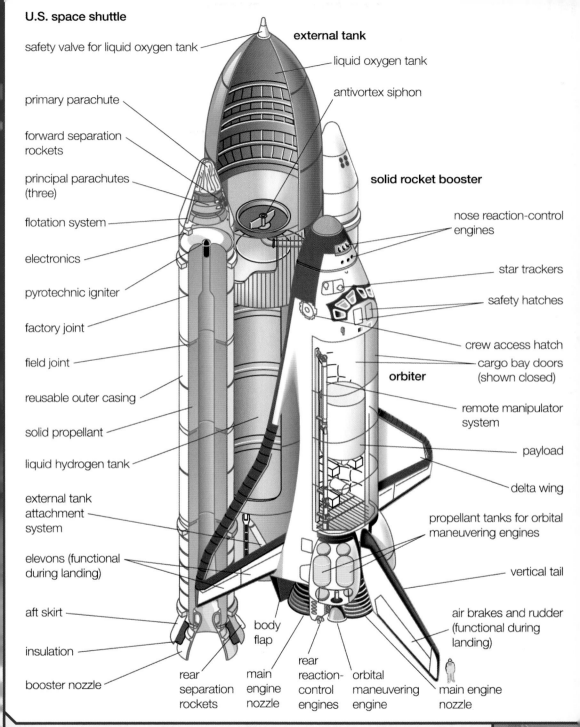

external tank

safety valve for liquid oxygen tank

liquid oxygen tank

antivortex siphon

primary parachute

forward separation rockets

principal parachutes (three)

flotation system

electronics

pyrotechnic igniter

factory joint

field joint

reusable outer casing

solid propellant

liquid hydrogen tank

external tank attachment system

elevons (functional during landing)

aft skirt

insulation

booster nozzle

solid rocket booster

nose reaction-control engines

star trackers

safety hatches

crew access hatch

cargo bay doors (shown closed)

orbiter

remote manipulator system

payload

delta wing

propellant tanks for orbital maneuvering engines

vertical tail

air brakes and rudder (functional during landing)

body flap

rear separation rockets

main engine nozzle

rear reaction-control engines

orbital maneuvering engine

main engine nozzle

The U.S. space shuttle was composed of a winged orbiter, an external liquid-propellant tank, and two solid-fuel rocket boosters.

The *Columbia* flew four orbital test flights during the period from April 1981 to July 1982. The first flight (STS 1) was flown by astronauts John W. Young and Robert Crippen. The next three flights carried payloads to demonstrate the shuttle's utility as a carrier. Beginning with the STS 5 in 1982, the shuttle carried operational payloads.

The shuttle *Challenger* made its first flight in April 1983. On its next ascent, in June, the crew included the first U.S. woman in space, Sally K. Ride. *Columbia* went up again in November carrying Spacelab 1, a highly complex laboratory module. In February 1984 astronauts Bruce McCandless II and Robert L. Stewart used gas-jet propulsion backpacks called manned maneuvering units (MMUs) to move and work in space and return to the shuttle *Challenger* while free of any lifeline to the spacecraft.

On January 28, 1986, after 24 successful launches, the shuttle *Challenger* exploded 73 seconds after liftoff. Its seven crew members were killed, including schoolteacher Christa McAuliffe, the winner of a nationwide teacher-in-space contest. The shuttle program was suspended until the exact cause of the explosion could be found. The United States returned to space in 1988 with the launching of

SALLY RIDE

In 1983 the astronaut Sally Ride became the first American woman to travel into space. Only two other women preceded her into space: Valentina Tereshkova (in 1963) and Svetlana Savitskaya (in 1982), both from the former Soviet Union.

Sally Kristen Ride was born on May 26, 1951, in Encino, California. She showed great early promise as a tennis player, but she eventually gave up her plans to play professionally and attended Stanford University. She graduated in 1973 with bachelor's degrees in English and physics. In 1978, as a doctoral candidate and teaching assistant in

(continued on the next page)

Sally Ride (1951–2012) serves as mission specialist on the flight deck of the space shuttle *Challenger*.

(continued from the previous page)

laser physics at Stanford, she was selected by the National Aeronautics and Space Administration (NASA) as one of six women astronaut candidates. Ride received a Ph.D. in astrophysics and began her training and evaluation courses that same year. In August 1979 she completed her NASA training, obtained a pilot's license, and became eligible for assignment as a U.S. space shuttle mission specialist.

On June 18, 1983, Ride became the first American woman in space while rocketing into orbit aboard the space shuttle *Challenger*. The shuttle mission lasted six days, during which time she helped deploy two communications satellites and carry out a variety of experiments. She served on a second space mission aboard *Challenger* in October 1984. The crew included another woman, Ride's childhood friend Kathryn Sullivan, who became the first American woman to walk in space.

Ride was training for a third shuttle mission when the *Challenger* exploded after launch in January 1986, a catastrophe that caused NASA to suspend shuttle flights for more than two years. Ride served on the presidential commission appointed to investigate the accident. She repeated that role as a member of the commission that investigated the in-flight breakup of the shuttle *Columbia* in February 2003.

Ride resigned from NASA in 1987, and in 1989 she became a professor of physics at the University of California, San Diego, and director of its California Space Institute (until 1996). In 1999–2000 she held executive positions with Space.com, a Web site presenting space, astronomy, and technology content. From the 1990s Ride initiated or headed a number of programs and organizations devoted to fostering science in education, particularly to providing support for schoolgirls interested in science, mathematics, or technology. She also wrote or collaborated on several children's books about space exploration and her personal experiences as an astronaut. Ride died in La Jolla, California, on July 23, 2012. In 2013 she was posthumously awarded the Presidential Medal of Freedom.

the space shuttle *Discovery* in September. The mission reflected hundreds of design changes. In 1991 the United States replaced the shuttle *Challenger* with the new *Endeavour*.

The 113th space shuttle mission ended in tragedy. On February 1, 2003, while returning from a 16-day scientific mission, *Columbia* broke apart about 40 miles (60 kilometers) above north-central Texas. Its crew of seven, including Ilan Ramon, the first Israeli astronaut to travel in space, died in the accident. It was the 28th mission for *Columbia*, which had been the oldest shuttle in the fleet.

The U.S. space shuttle program ended in 2011, some 30 years after the initial shuttle launch. The final space shuttle mission, the 135th, launched on July 8, 2011. *Atlantis* made the final flight.

The space shuttle *Atlantis* was launched on July 8, 2011, to begin the final space shuttle mission. The shuttle carried supplies and parts to the International Space Station.

The Soviet Union had launched a space shuttle, *Buran* (Blizzard), on an unmanned mission in November 1988. It completed two orbits of Earth. *Buran* was remarkably similar to the U.S. shuttle except for the design of the launch vehicle.

CHAPTER 6

INTERNATIONAL COOPERATION IN SPACE

Many organizations promote cooperation between the space agencies of countries around the world. These organizations range from international scientific bodies and national professional organizations to industrial concerns and amateur rocket societies.

International cooperation in the exploration of space takes many forms. These range from treaties that define the rights of spacefaring countries to genuine partnerships and exchanges of engineers and scientists on staffs and in academia. Cooperation has involved financial assistance, the donation of rockets and instruments, and the training of foreign scientists, technicians, and teachers in colleges and laboratories. Scientists foster the free exchange of ideas and the results of space research. Industrialists spur cooperation in space research and technology. They not only seek markets for space vehicles but also encourage the development of other

applications and markets for the materials and products of space research.

THE UNITED NATIONS AND OTHER INTERNATIONAL AGENCIES

Several organizations of the United Nations (UN) encourage international cooperation in space. The International Telecommunications Union allocates radio frequencies worldwide to avoid signal confusion and interference and assigns the orbital positions for various Earth satellites. The World Meteorological Organization, which sponsors the World Weather Watch, collects and distributes to all countries data from meteorological satellites, together with information gathered by sounding rockets, balloons, and ground-based observations.

The UN Educational, Scientific and Cultural Organization (UNESCO) concerns itself with scientific research, including research connected with space exploration. The World Health Organization finds many uses on Earth for medical knowledge gained in space research. The International Civil Aviation Organization seeks to eliminate the possibility that space vehicles leaving or entering Earth's atmosphere might interfere with or endanger civil aircraft.

Several international treaties have been approved through the UN to define acceptable conduct in space. The UN Space Treaty of 1967, for example, banned weapons of mass destruction from space and bound its signatories to return to the owner any spacecraft reentering over foreign territory. The country of origin is also bound to report launch details and to handle any damages resulting from its space operations.

There are several international space organizations in addition to the UN bodies. The European Launcher Development Organization (ELDO) built the Europa 1 launch vehicle, which combined a British first stage, a French second stage, a German third stage, and an Italian satellite. Belgium and the Netherlands provided supporting ground facilities, and early versions of the rocket were launched from Woomera, Australia.

The European Space Agency (ESA) was formed in 1976 by the merger of ELDO with

the European Space Research Organization (ESRO). ESA is engaged in both fundamental research and the development of spacecraft and missions. ESA has 22 member countries, and Canada also participates in some ESA projects. The agency developed the advanced Ariane family of launchers and the Spacelab laboratory module, which was carried aboard the U.S. space shuttle. ESA also built and launched the Giotto spacecraft, which flew close to the nucleus of Halley's comet in 1986. Its subsequent missions have included the infrared space telescope Herschel and probes sent to study the Sun, Mars, Venus, Saturn's moon Titan, and the cosmic microwave background radiation.

Most countries have their own space agencies. The size of these national agencies depends on the country's economic status and its stake in space. Indonesia, for example, has invested heavily in communications satellites as a means of tying together the many Indonesian islands. Japan's national space agency, the Japan Aerospace Exploration Agency (JAXA), was formed in 2003 by the merger of three institutions—the Institute of Space and Astronautical Sciences, the National Space Development Agency, and the

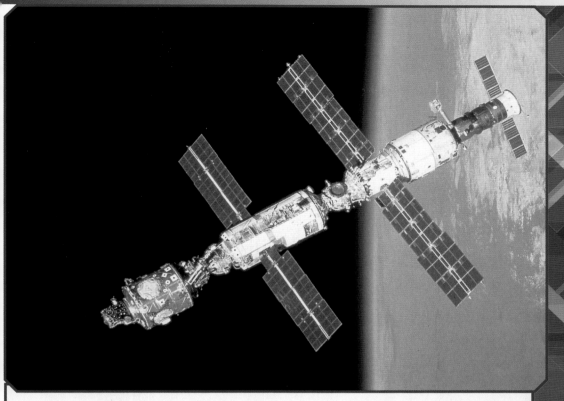

The International Space Station (ISS) program is a partnership between .the space agencies of numerous countries. The main participants are the United States, Russia, Japan, Canada, and countries of the European Space Agency.

National Aerospace Laboratory. Other major space agencies include the China National Space Administration (CNSA) and the Indian Space Research Organisation (ISRO).

In 1994 the Russian space agency joined NASA, ESA, Japan's National Space Development Agency, and the Canadian Space Agency in an agreement to build

INTERNATIONAL SPACE STATION

Assembly of the International Space Station began with the launches of the Russian control module Zarya on November 20, 1998, and the U.S.-built Unity connecting node the following month, which were linked in orbit by U.S. space shuttle astronauts. In mid-2000 the Russian-built module Zvezda, a habitat and control center, was added, and on November 2 of that year the ISS received its first resident crew, comprising two Russians and an American. A NASA microgravity laboratory called Destiny and other elements were subsequently joined to the station.

Russian modules were carried into space and docked to the ISS by Russian expendable launch vehicles. Other elements were ferried up by space shuttle and assembled in orbit during space walks. Both shuttles and Russian Soyuz spacecraft transported people to and from the station, and a Soyuz remained docked to the ISS at all times as a "lifeboat." Aside from the United States and Russia, station construction involved Canada, Japan, Brazil, and 11 ESA members.

After the breakup of the space shuttle *Columbia* in February 2003, the shuttle fleet was grounded, which effectively halted expansion of the station. Meanwhile, the crew was reduced from three to two, and their role was restricted mainly to caretaker status, limiting the amount of science that could be done. After the shuttle resumed regular flights in 2006, the ISS crew size was increased to three. Construction resumed in September of that year, with the addition of a pair of solar wings and a thermal radiator. The European-built American node, Harmony, was placed on the end of Destiny in October 2007.

Harmony has a docking port for the space shuttle and connecting ports for a European laboratory, Columbus, and a Japanese laboratory, Kibo. In February 2008 Columbus was mounted on Harmony's starboard side. In June 2008 the main part of Kibo was installed.

The ISS became fully operational in May 2009 when it began hosting a six-person crew. An external platform was attached to the far end of Kibo in July 2009, and a Russian docking port and airlock, Poisk, was attached to the Zvezda module in November 2009. A third node, Tranquility, was installed in 2010.

The space agencies that are partners in the ISS have not definitively decided when the program will end, but in 2010 the administration of U.S. President Barack Obama announced that the ISS program would continue "likely beyond 2020." In 2014 the Obama Administration indicated that the program would receive support until "at least 2024."

the International Space Station (ISS). The assembly of the ISS began in late 1998, when the first two components of the station were launched into space. A series of U.S. shuttle and Russian rocket launches carried up additional elements and equipment, and in November 2000 the first crew took up residence in the station.

OTHER ORGANIZATIONS

Many influential nonpolitical bodies further international cooperation in space. The International Telecommunications Satellite Consortium (Intelsat) was founded in 1964 by the telecommunication agencies of 18 countries, including the United States, to develop technologies for satellite communications. Intelsat became a private company in 2001.

Professional organizations are a significant avenue for developing both international and national space programs. National organizations that foster the free exchange of space information have been established in most of the countries of western Europe and the Americas and in Japan. The British Interplanetary Society, for example, has supported many theoretical studies of spaceflight. The American Institute of Aeronautics and Astronautics and the National Space Society in the United States, the SRON Netherlands Institute for Space Research, and a number of organizations in other countries provide meeting grounds for professionals to discuss space plans and findings. Under the auspices of the International Astronautical Federation, members of various national space organizations meet regularly.

In most countries—among others, the United States, Russia, Poland, Germany, France, Bulgaria, England, and Australia—there are also amateur rocket societies for young people. The members of such societies can learn about and experiment with space technology. Amateur groups in the United States and Australia, for instance, have constructed inexpensive but functional satellites that have been launched into space. Many future space scientists and astronauts will most likely come from clubs of this sort.

CONCLUSION

Space exploration and development have been stimulated by a complex mixture of motivations, including scientific inquiry, intense competition between national governments and ideologies, and commercial profit. Underlying them has been a vision of the outward movement of humans from Earth, ultimately leading to permanent settlements in space or on other celestial bodies. In reality, however, as of the early 21st century only 27 people had traveled beyond Earth orbit, all of them Apollo astronauts during the primarily politically inspired race to the Moon. Whether, and under what conditions, human exploration and settlement of the solar system will resume is a major issue for the future.

Scientists will continue to seek answers to leading questions about the physical and biological universe through the deployment of increasingly advanced instruments on orbiting satellites and space probes. The principal space-faring countries appear willing to continue their substantial support for space science. The availability of government funding will set the pace of scientific progress.

The various applications of space capability hold the greatest promise for significant change. If other commercial ventures equal or surpass the success of the satellite communications sector, space could become a major center of business activity. If governments decide to expand the activity in space of their armed forces, space could become another major military theater—like the land, the sea, and the air on Earth—for waging war and deploying weapons. If observing Earth from space becomes crucial for effective planetary management, an assortment of increasingly varied and specialized observation satellites could be launched. Thus, outer space could become a much busier area of human activity as the 21st century progresses.

GLOSSARY

ablative Of or related to removing or destroying especially by cutting, abrading, or evaporating.

apogee The point in outer space where an object traveling around Earth (such as a satellite or the Moon) is farthest away from Earth.

attitude The position of an aircraft or spacecraft determined by the relationship between its axes and a reference point (such as the horizon or a particular star).

ballistic Of or relating to the science that studies the movement of objects (such as bullets or rockets) that are shot or forced to move forward through the air.

centrifuge A machine that applies a sustained centrifugal force—that is, a force due to rotation. A human centrifuge is used in spaceflight training to get astronauts accustomed to acceleration forces they will experience in space.

cislunar Lying between Earth and the Moon or the Moon's orbit.

eccentricity A measure of an astronomical orbit's deviation from circularity.

ellipse A shape that resembles a flattened circle; oval.

geodetic Of or relating to geodesy, the science of measuring Earth.

inertia A property of matter by which something that is not moving remains still and something that is moving goes at the same speed and in the same direction until another thing or force affects it.

orthostatic Of, relating to, or caused by an upright posture.

payload The things (such as passengers or bombs) that are carried by an aircraft or spacecraft.

perigee The point in outer space where an object traveling around Earth (such as a satellite or the Moon) is closest to Earth.

posigrade Moving in the same direction as similar bodies.

primary The celestial body around which another celestial body or a satellite revolves.

propulsion The force that propels something, or moves it forward.

radiation A type of dangerous and powerful energy that is produced by radioactive substances and nuclear reactions.

reaction engine An engine that develops thrust by expelling a jet of fluid or a stream of particles.

retrograde Having or being motion in a direction contrary to that of similar bodies.

sidereal period The time required for a body in the solar system to complete one revolution with respect to the fixed stars — that is, as observed from some fixed point outside the system.

synodic period The time required for a body in the solar system to return to the same or approximately the same position relative to the Sun as seen by an observer on Earth.

telemeter To transmit data (such as pressure, speed, or temperature measurements) especially by radio to a distant station.

velocity The rate of change of position along a straight line with respect to time.

Canadian Space Agency (CSA)
John H. Chapman Space Centre
6767 Route de l'Aéroport
Saint-Hubert, QC J3Y 8Y9
Canada
(450) 926-4800
Website: http://www.asc-csa.gc.ca
The CSA oversees Canada's space program
and disseminates information about its
research to the public through its publi-
cations and outreach programs.

H.R. MacMillan Space Centre
1100 Chestnut Street
Vancouver, BC V6J 3J9
Canada
(604) 738-7827
Website: http://www.spacecentre.ca
The H.R. MacMillian Space Centre is a
nonprofit community resource based in
Vancouver, Canada. The Centre inspires
interest in the universe and space exploration through its programs and exhibits.

National Aeronautics and Space
Administration (NASA)

300 E Street SW, Suite 5R30
Washington, DC 20546
(202) 358-0001
Website: http://www.nasa.gov
NASA is a government agency that oversees
the U.S. space program. Its website provides information on its past and planned
missions, including preparations for a
journey to Mars.

National Air and Space Museum
Independence Avenue at 6th Street SW
Washington, DC 20560
(202) 633-2214
Website: http://www.nasm.si.edu
The National Air and Space Museum's
extensive collection of artifacts, including historic aircraft and spacecraft,
recounts the history of aviation and
space travel.

The Planetary Society
60 South Los Robles Avenue
Pasadena, CA 91101
(626) 793-5100
Website: http://planetary.org
The Planetary Society educates the public
on the benefits of space exploration and

provides funding for space research and the development of space technology.

U.S. Space and Rocket Center
One Tranquility Base
Huntsville, AL 35805
(800) 63-SPACE
Website: http://www.rocketcenter.com
The U.S. Space and Rocket Center houses one of the largest collections of rockets and space artifacts in the world and chronicles the history of the U.S. space program. It also runs the Space Camp and Space Academy for students.

WEBSITES

Because of the changing nature of internet links, Rosen Publishing has developed an online list of websites related to the subject of this book. This site is updated regularly. Please use this link to access this list:

http://www.rosenlinks.com/SCI/space

Anderson, Michael, ed. *Pioneers in Astronomy and Space Exploration.* New York, NY: Britannica Educational Publishing, 2013.

Barbree, John. *Neil Armstrong: A Life of Flight.* New York, NY: Thomas Dunne Books, 2014.

Bortz, Fred. *The Big Bang Theory: Edwin Hubble and the Origins of the Universe.* New York, NY: Rosen Publishing, 2014.

Brezina, Corona. *Newly Discovered Planets: Is There Potential for Life?* New York, NY: Rosen Publishing, 2016.

Dickmann, Nancy. *Exploring Beyond the Solar System.* New York, NY: Rosen Publishing, 2015.

Hasan, Heather, ed. *How Mathematical Models, Computer Simulations, and Exploration Can Be Used to Study the Universe.* New York, NY: Rosen Publishing, 2006.

Hollar, Sherman, ed. *Astronomy: Understanding the Universe.* New York, NY: Britannica Educational Publishing, 2012.

Hollar, Sherman, ed. *The Inner Planets: Mercury, Venus, and Mars.* New York,

NY: Britannica Educational Publishing, 2012.

Hollar, Sherman, ed. *The Outer Planets: Jupiter, Saturn, Uranus, and Neptune.* New York, NY: Britannica Educational Publishing, 2012.

Sherr, Lynn. *Sally Ride: America's First Woman in Space.* New York, NY: Simon & Schuster, 2014.

Sparrow, Giles, Judith John, and Chris McNab, eds. *Exploring Space.* New York, NY: Cavendish Square, 2016.

Sparrow, Giles, Judith John, and Chris McNab, eds. *Shuttles and Space Missions.* New York, NY: Cavenidish Square, 2016.

Tyson, Neil deGrasse. *Space Chronicles: Facing the Ultimate Frontier.* New York, NY: W.W. Norton, 2012.

INDEX